THE
Archive Photographs
SERIES

NORTHFIELD

THE
Archive Photographs
SERIES

NORTHFIELD

Compiled by
Pauline Caswell

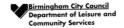
Birmingham City Council
Department of Leisure and
Community Services

CHALFORD

First published 1996
Copyright © Pauline Caswell, 1996

The Chalford Publishing Company
St Mary's Mill, Chalford,
Stroud, Gloucestershire, GL6 8NX

ISBN 0 7524 0679 5

Typesetting and origination by
The Chalford Publishing Company
Printed in Great Britain by
Redwood Books, Trowbridge

Contents

Acknowledgements

My thanks go to the Local Studies and History Section of Birmingham Reference Library, for the use of their collection of photographs and to Robert Ryland for his assistance.

The collection of photographs in Northfield Library were also made available to me and I would like to thank especially Peter Richards, Margaret Scott, Alison Gawith and all those who have donated pictures to the library collection.

I am also grateful for access to the Northfield Society display material which includes photographs given to the Society by Jean and Mary Banton.

Betty Prettyman, Margaret Lane, Greta Baldwin, Dorothy Hargest and Stuart Andrew have all offered me photographs and background information.

Introduction

Northfield or 'Nordfeld' was a settlement in North Worcestershire owned by the Saxon landowner Aelfwold, but in 1086, when the Domesday survey was completed Nordfeld had been placed by the King, along with thirteen other Worcestershire manors, under the Lordship of a Norman knight, William Fitz-Ansculf. William came to the area from the Picardie region of France and in 1086 held estates in eleven English counties among them manors in Worcestershire and Warwickshire including Northfield, Frankley, Cradley, Pedmore, Hagley, Weoley, Edgbaston, Aston and Handsworth. Although William had a castle in Dudley, each of the manors had its own manor house, Northfield's would have been close to the church on land we now know as Old Moat Drive. In the Domesday Survey, Northfield was described as having six hides (90 acres) under cultivation with the Lord of the Manor having as much as can be worked by one plough solely for his own use, and living in the village one priest, seven villeins, sixteen bordars, six cottars who shared enough land for thirteen ploughs to work, also two serfs and one bondswoman (a slave). This has been calculated as a population of around 130, and indeed it remained a small rural community until relatively recently.

St Laurence church was not built until the middle of the twelfth century although there was a priest in Northfield in Saxon times. The church was most likely built with stone brought from the quarry in Quarry Lane and would have originally consisted of only the nave and the chancel. The church has been enlarged over the centuries, with the south aisle added in the fourteenth century and a north aisle in 1899. There are many interesting features such as the Norman doorway, the 'lepers squint' and a hidden staircase. The churchyard extends behind the cottages on Church Hill until it meets the 'Darkie', a footpath that joins Church Hill crossing the railway line, with Wychall Road.

The Great Stone Inn, a Medieval building, stands opposite the church, next to the village 'pound' where, in past centuries, stray animals were tethered. These are the oldest remaining buildings in Northfield, and explain the quote, 'Northfield, where at the Great Stone Inn beer is sold by the Pound…'

The Bristol Road has always been an important highway and in the seventeenth century it was a narrow, stoney road full of pot-holes, it was described at the time as '…impassable for waggons and carriages and very dangerous for horses laden and travellers…'. After the section through Northfield became a Turnpike Road in 1762 it was repaired but still remained dangerous and was notorious for accidents. In the spring of 1766 the Bristol mail coach overturned near the Bell and the guard was killed. Today the road, the A38, is a very busy one leading directly to the M5, but despite the congestion the road has a deserved reputation as being the leafiest and most attractive of the city's main roads.

The greatest change in Northfield must have been the coming of the railway and although work started on the line in the 1840s the station was not opened until 1870. To celebrate the opening of the station a group of local businessmen met for dinner in the Bell Inn and discussed the new commercial opportunities a railway station made possible. One of the local businessmen, Charles Pegram, built houses in Station Road for railway workers and he soon added a roller skating rink and a Temperance Hotel close to the station. In the First World War the skating rink was used to manufacture hand grenades but, after an accident, a fire destroyed the rink and it was never replaced.

Until the nineteenth century the main living in Northfield was to be had from the land, as its many farms and corn mills alongside the River Rea illustrate. The only industry was nail making, carried out in small workshops behind the cottages near the church, but the coming of the railway also heralded the expansion of local industry. In a short time three major employers moved into or close to Northfield. In 1879 the Cadbury Brothers decided to build their Garden Factory in Bournville, Herbert Austin founded the Austin Works at Longbridge in 1905 and in 1908 Oliver Morland and F. Paul Impey opened their Kalamazoo factory in Northfield. These new industries were to have a major influence on the growth of Northfield in providing work for large number of people but also for the influence their founders had on the lives of their workers and the neighbourhood. George Cadbury, Herbert Austin and F. Paul Impey and their families were all very active and generous in providing the area with new houses, parks, and a library. Two of George Cadbury's sons, George and Edward, provided money to enable the Birmingham Association for the Preservation of Open Spaces, to purchase Rednal Hill in 1899, part of the Lickey Hills, a favourite day out by tram in pre-war times, and still popular today. It was George Cadbury who bought the house, The Woodlands, and in 1909 gave it to the Crippled Children's Union for use as a hospital. George and his wife Dame Elizabeth Cadbury were regular hospital visitors and very involved in charitable work.

In 1911, Northfield became part of Birmingham and the Kings Norton and Northfield Urban District Council ceased to exist. Gradually Northfield lost its rural identity as it became part of a big city. Between the wars and again in the 1950s and 1960s there was a boom in house building with the City Council building several large council estates and the first blocks of flats. At the same time Bournville Village Trust developed a large area of land to the west of the Bristol Road.

The farms and the mills may have gone now that the land has been redeveloped but there still remains a number of parks and a great many trees. In an attempt to preserve some of Northfield's old buildings conservation area status was given to part of Northfield in 1971, when local residents campaigned to save the old school from demolition. This area contains St Laurence church, the Old School, the Great Stone Inn, Village Pound and the nailers' cottages and recently the same status has been given to the Austin Village an estate of wooden bungalows built by Herbert Austin in 1916.

Anyone interested in finding out more about the area will find that the Local Studies and History Section of the Central Library has a large collection of photographs and material relating to the history and growth of Northfield, also the Archives Section holds the Northfield Survey Group's collection of material collected during the 1950s. Local community libraries also have information and Northfield Library has a collection of photographs, maps and newscuttings.

One
The Village

Bell Lane *c.* 1903, at its junction with Bristol Road South. The shop in the centre of the picture was a butchers and on the right was a bakers shop. The tree on the right hand corner was later replaced by Huins shoe shop and although it is now a travel agency, the junction is still known to local people as Huins corner.

Northfield on a winter's day in 1904. Note the thin coating of snow over the pavements.

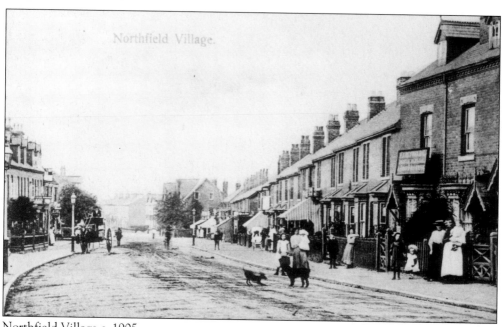

Northfield Village *c.* 1905.

The Bristol Road South and Church Road junction *c.* 1900. In the centre of the picture Ash Bank Farm can be seen, next to the Bell Hotel. On the opposite corner was the village blacksmith's house and workshop.

The Toll House on Bristol Road South c. 1900. The Bristol Road became a turnpike road in 1762.

The Old Malt House where beer was brewed and supplied to the Red Lion later known as Elm cottage. In later years the malt house was used for meetings. Alongside, a row of cottages were built as an extension to the original malthouse, but all these have now been demolished. The Job Centre is now on the site of the malt house.

Frank Hands grocery business on the corner of Chatham Road in 1897. The shop was started in 1895 but was still in business in the 1930s and is remembered by many Northfield residents. Compare this photograph with the one on page 19.

The corner of Bell Lane *c.* 1910, showing Edward Lee's greengrocery shop on the left and the butchers shop next door set back from the road. These buildings are among the oldest buildings in Northfield although their use has changed over the years.

The village smithy on the corner of Church Road. This corner became known later as Tay's Corner because between the 1930s and 1960s a number of shops were opened by Joseph Tay. Today the site of the blacksmiths shop is covered by a car park and bus stops.

The residents of Northfield gather together on the Bristol Road – but what for?

15

The Davis Drapery shops, on Bristol Road South, next to Huins shoe shop, *c.* 1930.

The corner of Bristol Road South and Bells Lane, *c.* 1910, with the new shoe shop on the corner – James Huins, Bootmaker.

Northfield Village *c.* 1915, showing the junction of Bristol Road South with Church Road and Bell Lane.

Northfield Village looking north *c.* 1920. The telegraph pole on the right is where Woolworth's is today.

The blacksmith's house, *c. 1923*, on the corner of Church Road. The house was demolished in 1935.

Bristol Road junction, looking north, 1922.

One of the first Austin Sevens to be produced, standing outside Frank Hands grocery shop in July 1922. This photograph was taken to advertise the car and shows Mr Hands loading the car. The shop was on the corner of Chatham Road and today it is an Insurance Brokers.

The shopping centre on the Bristol Road South, c. 1930, looking north. The corner on the right of the photograph is now Lloyds bank corner.

The Northfield shopping centre, Bristol Road South c. 1940, looking towards the city.

Northfield cinema on the Bristol Road South, *c.* 1930. This cinema was built by the Hodge brothers in 1929 and opened the week after the first 'talkie' had been shown in the city centre. The cinema was demolished in the 1960s and replaced by a supermarket. The indoor market now stands on this spot.

The junction of Cock Lane (now Frankley Beeches Road) and Bristol Road South 1935. On the right hand edge of the photograph was the 'Old Methodist Chapel'. On the triangular island Ernest Loxley had a monumental stone masonry business

The corner of Cock Lane, 1934, showing the Black Horse public house and the corner shop. The sign in front of the cars advertises trips to see Aston Villa, for a shilling.

Northfield looking towards the south, c. 1940, with Wheeler's garage on the left and opposite, next to Barnes Bakery.

The 'Bell' crossroads, 1952.

These properties on the Bristol Road South, were all demolished to make way for the Grosvenor Shopping Centre. The cottage on the left sold flowers and greengrocery (Singletons) and between the two cafes was a shoemaker and repairer, (Mills). Rookery Nook was a gaming house and early form of amusement arcade.

A charity event in Northfield, c. 1960, showing the shops on Tays corner. There have been a great many changes to these shops in recent years.

24

Two
Roads to the Church

Church Road, *c.* 1910, between what is now Maas Road and Great Stone Road. The bank of trees on the left were just below the library.

Church Road in the snow, *c.* 1930. This is just outside the library.

Northfield library, Church Road. This photograph was taken in 1913. The library was first opened in September 1906.

The Interior of Northfield Library, 1913.

The library after a fire in 1914. The library was reputed to have been burnt down by local suffragettes. A paper was found on the railings at the rear saying, 'Give Women the Vote' and a parcel containing a book by Christabel Pankhurst with a note which read, 'To start your new library'.

The Fire Brigade until 1911, was a volunteer force and had its station at 146 Maas Road. This photograph was taken in the field at the rear of Northfield Institute, where the brigade regularly practised. The building behind them was the old band room. The firemen pictured are, Charlie Hodgetts, Harry Taylor, Sammy Stokes the driver and Jack Hunt the captain. In 1911 Northfield became part of Birmingham and the brigade became part of the city force. They continued to use the Maas Road station until the new station was built in 1959 on the corner of South Road. Northfield brigade continued to use horses until 1918 after which they switched to motor tenders. When the library was on fire in 1914, Mr E. Jinks, who lived in a cottage opposite, spotted the flames and ran up Maas Road to call out the brigade, but the fire was too great for them to cope with and Kings Heath brigade was called out as well.

The Nailers Cottages (Street Cottages) on Church Road, *c.* 1930. These were demolished in 1964 when Great Stone Road was opened up for through traffic.

Street Cottages, *c.* 1960, when Church Road was widened at its junction with Bunbury Road.

Church Road junction with Bunbury Road, c. 1930. On the corner is the end wall of Street Cottages and opposite the junction is Street Farm.

Street farm on the start of Bunbury Road. This was demolished in the late 1960s and replaced by the YMCA building.

Bunbury Road and Church Road junction, 1934.

Bunbury Road and Woodland Road junction, c. 1935.

Bunbury Road, *c.* 1920. The white gates belong to Middleton Farm. This is now the position of Knighton Road.

Bunbury Road, *c.* 1930, looking towards the junction with Middleton Hall Road.

32

eat Stone Inn & Pound, Northfield.

The Great Stone Inn and Pound, Northfield, *c.* 1900. A 'pound' or 'pinfold' was used to tether stray animals. The animals were seized and impounded by the 'pinder' and kept in the pound until claimed by their owners who would have to pay a fine to obtain their release. Ancient records show a variety of strays held – bulls, oxen, cows, horses, pigs, a boar and a swarm of bees!

The Great Stone Inn and Pound, 1936.

The Pound, alongside the Great Stone Inn. This photograph was taken in the 1920s.

Church Hill viewed from Rectory Road with the churchyard on the left, and Great Stone Inn on the right, c. 1936.

Church Hill viewed from the station drive, showing Beech Farm.

The interior of No. 9, Church Hill, in the late 1930s. Note the bread oven.

Three
St Laurence Church
and School

St Laurence Church and the Great Stone Inn, 1941. The large stone on the corner was later moved into the pound as the traffic on this road increased and more recently the road has been made one-way.

Dinah Withers, outside the porch of
St Laurence church, c. 1890. Withers is
an old Northfield name and appears
often in the parish registers. It has been
suggested that Dinah Withers was the
local midwife.

A May Day procession held, c. 1900, on land near the church. The two teachers were Mabel
Hunt and Ada Morris.

The curate of St Laurence in
November 1895.

St Laurence church steps 1908. Gladys Woodbine is the little girl on the steps with her brother
Frank. The couple standing by the wall are her parents. On the left is the wall of the old school
and the Nailers Cottages.

St Laurence church, 1924, with scaffolding round the tower. The tower was thoroughly restored in 1924. The sign on the scaffolding shows that 'Sapcotes' was the firm that carried out the restoration.

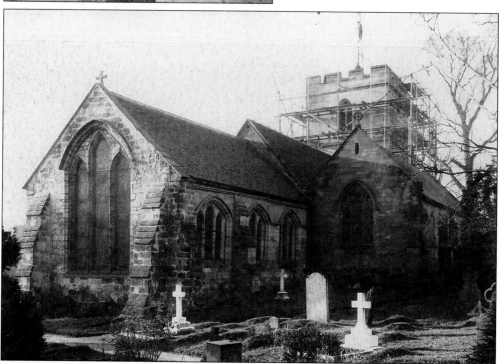

St Laurence church viewed from the east of the churchyard showing the chancel and north aisle which was added during the nineteenth century.

Northfield church cross was erected in the churchyard in 1880 as a memorial to Revd Henry Clark, a former rector of St Laurence.

The interior of St Laurence church in August 1941, showing the screen made by local craftsmen and presented to the church in 1863 by Mr T.S. Stock who lived in The Priory (then known as Gainsborough House).

The 'leper's squint', in the wall of St Laurence church, viewed here from inside the chancel. There are no records of lepers in Northfield and this window was probably, therefore, intended to enable people outside the church to hear the bell being rung for communion.

Northfield church bell ringers, c. 1923, with the rector, Revd R.A. Haysom and Curate Revd J.E.E. Davies. Also in the group is Mr J. Parker (churchwarden), Jack Withers, Mr J. Bond, Mr Williamson and Fred Hobbis.

NORTHFIELD PARISH CHURCH, WORCS.
PEAL OF SIX RECAST AND TWO TREBLES TO COMPLETE PEAL
TENOR 14 CWT 1QR 13 LBS
TAYLORS, BELLFOUNDERS, LOUGHBOROUGH.

New bells were recast in 1924 and two more bells were added to make a peal of eight. The bells were rung for the first time on 22 December 1924. The first bell bears the inscription, 'We are now six, though once were five' and on one of the newer bells, 'I to the church the living call and to the grave do summon all'.

Lord and Lady Austin with Revd Haysom attending the dedication service for the new organ. The new organ was installed in 1937 and was the gift of Lord and Lady Austin.

Northfield church choir outside Church Cottage in 1924.

The Northfield church choir, c. 1927.

The Old Rectory, photographed from the top of the church tower by the rector's wife, Mrs Witton, *c.* 1920.

The curate's house, on land adjacent to the churchyard known locally as the 'Jungle'. The house was demolished and replaced by Bishop's Court. This priest's house became very dilapidated and damp over the years and was known as the 'Haunted House'.

St Laurence school across the road from the church. When the school was replaced by a new building on Bunbury Road, local residents campaigned successfully to save the Old school from demolition. Conservation area status was also achieved for the area surrounding the church.

The boys of St Laurence school in the playground, *c.* 1920.

The boys of St Laurence school, *c.* 1873.

The staff of St Laurence school, *c.* 1925. Clockwise, from the top left: Mr Stone, Mr Sage (headmaster), Mr Court, Mr Cook, Mrs Delahay and Miss Hill.

The teaching staff of St Laurence school, including Mr Sage (headmaster) in the centre, Mrs Delahay on the left and Mr Stone and Mr Court, each end of back row.

The boys of St Laurence school, c. 1930. Robert Sage, son of the headmaster, is second from the left in the second row. He later became a consultant surgeon at Selly Oak hospital.

One of the girl's classes of 1938 at St Laurence school.

A children's nativity play.

Four
Around the Station

Church Hill, c. 1895, before Woodland Road had been cut through the trees on the right. The house on the left was used by the stationmaster. Behind the house is Beech Farm and St Laurence school.

Horse-drawn taxis arrive at Northfield station. The station noticeboard has an advertisement for T. Wheeler, Cabs and Cars of Bristol Road. Wheeler's garage can be seen in photographs of Northfield Village.

A joke postcard sent to announce arrival in Northfield.

The Northfield railway station *c.* 1900. The station was first opened in September 1870.

A joke postcard to send on leaving Northfield.

A goods train pulls into Northfield station *c.* 1900.

Northfield station platform, *c.* 1910, showing roofs in Church Hill and Middlemore Road. Until the 1970s the platforms and booking office were nearer to Church Hill than they are now and local trains stopped either side of the central platform.

A horse-drawn coal wagon delivering to cottages on Church Hill.

The bridge at the junction of West Heath Road and Church Hill, *c.* 1910. On the left behind the tree is the roller skating rink built by Charles Pegram and opened on 11 November 1909. During the First World War it was converted to produce hand grenades, but there was an accident and a fire gutted the building. In more recent times this was a builders merchant, Perrins and Jones, but is now Atkinson's new premises.

The interior of the skating rink, *c.* 1910, with a refreshment bar at the rear.

TRAIN SERVICE.

	a.m.	a.m.	a.m.	p.m.	p.m.	p.m.	p.m.	p.m.
Birmingham ...	9 55	10 55	1 55	2 10	5 50	6 40	7 37	7 48
Five Ways ...	...	...	...		...	...	...	...
Church Road ...	...	...	...	Sats. only	...	...	...	...
Somerset Road ...	...	...	...		...	...	...	...
Selly Oak ...	...	...	...		6 0	...	...	...
Bournville ...	...	...	...		6 3	6 51	...	...
Camp Hill ...	...	...	2 4	2 18	...	...	...	...
Brighton Road ...	...	...	...	2 22	...	...	...	...
Moseley ...	...	...	...	2 25	...	...	...	...
Kings Heath ...	...	...	...	2 30	...	...	...	...
Hazelwell ...	...	...	...	2 35	...	...	...	...
Lifford ...	...	...	2 13	2 38	...	...	...	...
Kings Norton ...	10 7	11 10	2 16	2 41	6 7	6 55	7 49	8 0
Northfield ...	10 12	11 15	2 21	2 46	6 12	6 59	7 53	8 4

	p.m.	p.m.	p.m.	p.m.	p.m.	p.m.	p.m.	p.m.
Northfield ...	1 42	3 12	3 34	5 19	...	9 0	9 25	10 12
Kings Norton ...	1 46	3 17	3 39	5 23	5 40	9 5	9 29	10 16
Lifford ...	1 49	...	3 42	5 26	...	9 33	...	...
Hazelwell ...	1 52	...	3 45	5 29	...	9 37	10 21	
Kings Heath ...	1 55	...	3 48	5 32	...	9 40	10 24	
Moseley ...	1 58	...	3 51	5 35	...	9 45	10 27	
Brighton Road ...	2 1	...	3 54	5 38	...	9 46	10 30	
Camp Hill ...	2 5	...	3 57	5 42	...	9 51	10 35	
Bournville ...	...	...	...	...	5 45	9 9	...	...
Selly Oak ...	...	...	...	...	5 48	9 12	...	...
Somerset Road ...	...	...	...	...	5 51	9 16	...	...
Church Road ...	...	...	...	...	...	...	...	...
Five Ways ...	...	...	...	...	5 55	9 22	...	...
Birmingham ...	2 13	3 35	4 5	5 50	5 59	9 26	10 3	10 45

	a.m.	a.m.	p.m.	p.m.	p.m.	p.m.	p.m.	p.m.
Redditch ...	9 36	11 35	2 8	3 12	5 57	6 54	...	8 38
Alvechurch ...	9 45	11 44	2 17	3 21	6 6	7 3	...	8 48
Barnt Green ...	9 51	11 50	5 3	3 27	6 20	7 14	7 42	8 53
Northfield ...	9 58	11 57	3 12	3 34	6 27	7 21	7 49	9 0

	p.m.	p.m.	p.m.	p.m.	p.m.	p.m.	p.m.	p.m.
Northfield ...	12 37	12 55	1 17	4 25	5 20	9 0	9 38	10 42
Barnt Green ...	12 44	1 3	1 23	4 34	5 28	9 6	9 45	10 51
Alvechurch ...	12 49	Sats	...	4 39	5 33	...	9 50	...
Redditch ...	12 56	only	...	4 46	5 40	...	9 57	11 4

Frequent Service of Trams to Kings Norton.

This railway timetable and advertisement for Northfield roller rink was in the form of a postcard and gives us not only the admission price but a description of the rink, *c.* 1910.

The view along Station Road with the railway embankment on the right. The houses were built for railway workers and a tunnel constructed under the line in 1892 to allow easy access. The tunnel is still in daily use.

This view towards the railway bridge is from outside the roller skating rink in West Heath Road. The rink was built by Mr Charles Pegram after the railway line and station were completed. Its full title was Northfield Skating Rink and Winter Garden.

58

West Heath Road and Station Road junction, c. 1910. On the right on the corner of Station Road, above the shops, Charles Pegram opened a Temperance hotel.

The shop, now the post office, on the corner of Middlemore Road, c. 1950s.

Floods in West Heath Road, 3 May 1908. On the left is Staple Hall Road and the bend in West Heath Road, south of the junction, is known locally as the Ducks Elbow. This is named after the inn, of the same name, that stood on the spot in earlier times. The inn, a half timbered building, not only provided beer but also had a bowling alley.

Floods in West Heath Road in 1927. This is the present site of the Old Mill public house.

Five
At Leisure

The Church of England Working Mens Society band, c. 1890. This photograph was taken in the St Laurence school yard.

Northfield Silver Band, *c.* 1910, marching through Northfield. On the right is Elm Cottage, formerly the Red Lion public house, this was demolished fairly recently and replaced by shops.

The Children's Fete, 18 August 1908, this was an annual event. The procession has just reached the junction of Church Road and Bristol Road. Ash Bank Farm is on the right and on the left is a sign advertising the Cyclists Arms Coffee House, which was one of the early uses of Northfield Institute.

The Children's Fete procession in 1908, on the Bristol Road. This annual event, which attracted families from Birmingham to join in the fun, included a fancy dress competition. The procession would finish in Green Close an open area in Maas Road.

The head of the fete procession, 1908.

The Coronation procession of 1911, in South Road.

Mrs Parks was a well known and popular person in Northfield and is seen here planting a tree to commemorate the visit of Edward VII to Birmingham on the 7 July 1909.

Coronation celebrations in 1911.

The fancy dress entrants in the coronation celebrations of 1911. The celebrations took place in Green Close which was an open area between Maas Road and Bristol Road, and was frequently used for local events.

The Northfield Prize Silver Band of 1922.

Coronation celebrations around the bandstand in Victoria Common (Northfield Park), 1911.

Part of the Coronation procession, 1911, showing several prams that have been decorated for the occasion.

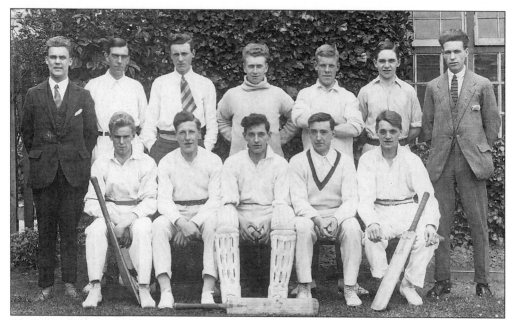

The Northfield Institute cricket team, *c.* 1922.

The Northfield Institute football team, 1922-3.

The fete procession outside Northfield Institute in 1908. The institute, built in 1892 by George Cadbury, was used as a meeting place for the Society of Friends (Quakers), and as an adult school. It was also a village coffee tavern known as the Cyclists Arms. As well as a meeting room for 700 people, it had a skittle alley and a billiard room. It was here in 1914 that Christabel Pankhurst addressed a meeting of local Suffragettes. The first caretakers, Mr and Mrs Hill, also ran Northfield's first post office in the adjoining building which is now a second-hand bookshop.

The marquee, erected in Green Close, Maas Road in 1908 for the annual fete.

The Northfield Church Amateur Operatic Society. Productions of *Tom Jones* on Tuesday 6 May 1930, and *San Toy* on Tuesday 23 April 1929.

The Geisha, a production by the Northfield Church Amateur Operatic Society, running from Tuesday 28 April to Saturday 2 May 1936. The producer and musical director of this, and the productions shown on the previous page, was the Rev R.A. Haysom, with music from the St Laurence Orchestra and Mr J.W. Peace on the piano. All the productions took place in the old Church Hall with admission at 2/6d (reserved seat) and 1/3d. The review in the local newspaper praised the music and the singing. A number of the cast were mentioned and praised for their performance, Mr A.W. Fellows, Miss F.M. Harper, Miss L.M. Peace and Mr J.P. Williamson.

King George V public house on the corner of Tessall Lane.

Old Bell House was situated at the junction of Bell Lane and Bell Holloway. The building dated back to the Queen Anne period and was first known as the Bell and Bluebell Inn. In the days of the stagecoach it was a coaching station midway between the Hen and Chickens in Birmingham and the Rose and Crown at the Lickeys. After a new Bell Inn was built in 1803-4, on the re-routed Bristol Road, the Old Bell became a private house until its demolition.

Luke Loud, a carpenter from Selly Oak, and friends photographed outside the Bell Hotel in 1895.

The Bell Inn, Northfield built in the 1890s, was the second Bell on this site. It was demolished in 1983 and replaced by a smaller public house and a number of shops.

The Old Black Horse, photographed just before it was replaced in 1924.

The new Black Horse under construction with the old one still alongside.

The builders at work on the new Black Horse.

New and Old Black Horse, Northfield.

Two Black Horses on the Bristol Road 1924. In fact there have been three public houses called the Black Horse on this site, here we see the second and third.

"Black Horse," Bristol Road South, Northfield.

The completed Black Horse. A brochure or guide to the new pub was published in 1929. In this the building was described in very glowing terms 'When I first saw the Black Horse I admit I was spellbound... such magnificence, yet such calm dignity, such beauty of line and contour an expressive poem in stone and wood'.

Northfield Swimming Baths exterior, *c.* 1940.

The interior of the swimming baths, *c.* 1940.

The Bristol Road with the Old Travellers Rest on the left, *c.* 1910.

The new Travellers Rest built originally with a thatched roof which was later replaced by tiles, 1926.

Six
The Woodlands Hospital

The Royal Orthopaedic Hospital, the Woodlands, opened in 1909 as a convalescent home for crippled children. This photograph, c. 1930, shows the tram lines in the centre of the road.

When a surgeon was appointed in 1914 this conservatory became the first operating theatre.

In 1912, a school was established at the hospital as many of the children could expect to be in the hospital for years rather than months. The school was recognised by the Board of Education in 1914, and was one of the first hospital schools in the Midlands.

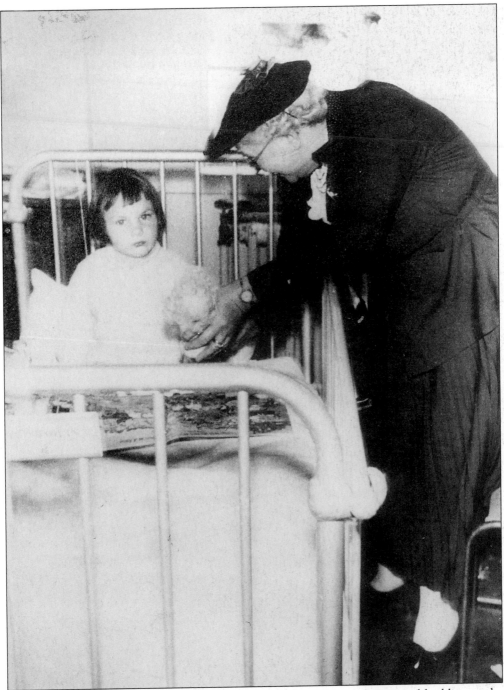

The hospital was established in 1909 when George Cadbury gave the original building to the Birmingham and District Crippled Children's Union for use as a convalescent home. Dame Elizabeth Cadbury who lived in the Manor House on the opposite side of the Bristol Road, visited the children in the Woodlands nearly everyday, she often brought her parrot or a donkey to amuse the children. On Sundays, George Cadbury visited and brought with him a bar of chocolate for each child.

George and Elizabeth Cadbury on their Silver Wedding Anniversary, 19 June 1913. This photograph was taken in the Girls' Garden opposite the Concert Hall in Bournville Lane.

The Rotarians sponsored all the treatment of children in these wards. The wards were open air for TB patients, who slept out of doors all year round with just a roof for protection. *c.* 1928.

The first ambulance at the Woodlands, *c.* 1920.

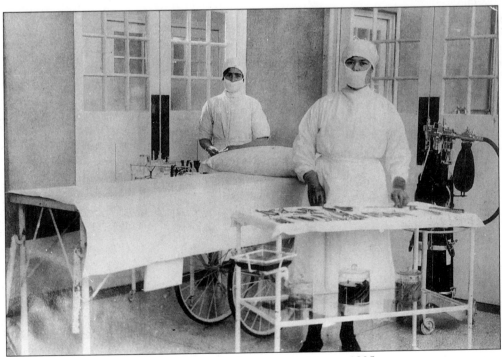

Nurses preparing the operating theatre, for the next operation, *c.* 1925.

On 6 November 1929, the Duke and Duchess of York, later George VI and Queen Elizabeth, opened the new buildings at the Woodlands. An appeal had been launched early in 1927 in order to raise money for extensions to allow for patients to be transferred from the Newhall Street building to Northfield. The extension comprised a children's ward, two adult wards, new operating theatres, a massage department and a gymnasium. There were also a number of improvements made to the kitchens and staff accommodation. The original estimate for the improvements was £24,481 but this did not include equipment and further appeals were made for this and for redecorating the existing building. In the photograph the Duchess of York is accompanied by Dame Elizabeth Cadbury as she tours a new ward.

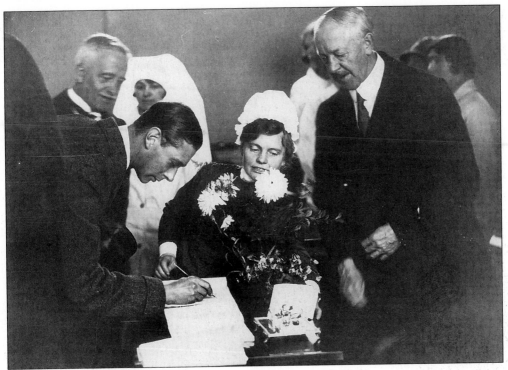

The Duke of York, George VI, signs the visitors book.

One of the new open air wards built on the site of the old stables, *c.* 1930.

A procession through Northfield to raise funds for the Woodlands Hospital.

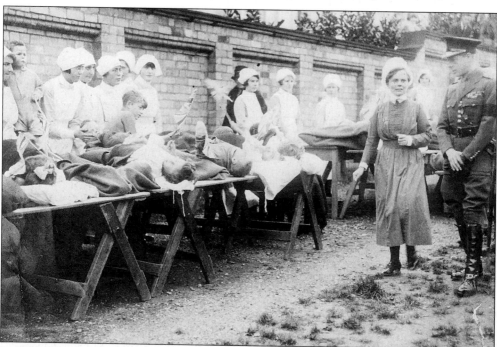

In 1933, the Prince of Wales, later the Duke of Windsor, visited the Woodlands Hospital, and patients and staff lined up along the Bristol Road. Matron Fanny Smith accompanied the Prince as he met the patients.

A Coronation Day party on the childrens' ward, June 1953.

The Northfield Children's Carnival, an annual event, always visited the hospital to show the costumes to the patients. These are the participants in the 1938 procession.

The matron, nurses and young patients display the gifts given to the hospital by local people to raise money to sponsor the 'Waterloo bed' in September 1933. Many local clubs, public houses and businesses sponsored beds in the hospital, and local families and sunday school classes collected groceries and eggs and took them along to the hospital each week for the young patients.

Seven
Northfield Churches

Two Methodist churches. The new church was completed, *c.* 1959 but has since been reduced in size and the main doors are now on Chatham Road. This site next door to the swimming baths is now a car spares and servicing business.

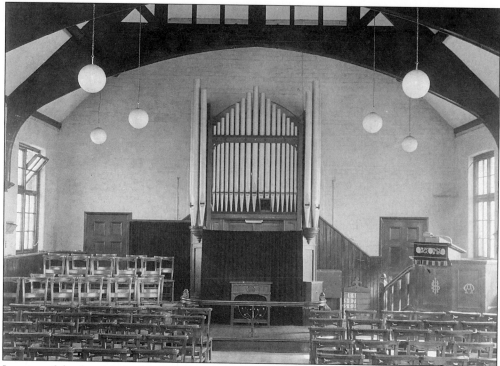

Interior of the first Methodist church, demolished, *c.* 1959.

Northfield Methodist church annual outing, 1914.

The Priory, on the Bristol Road, next to Woodlands Hospital, was originally called Gainsborough House and was built as the home of the Stocks family in 1862.

The rear of the Priory, the Convent of Our Lady of Charity, and the St Mary's home for Women and Girls. The convent was reduced in size, c. 1980 and Maryland Drive was built.

The Girl's Chapel, part of the Convent of Our Lady of Charity.

The original Longbridge Baptist church in Hawkesley Crescent.

The interior of St Brigids church, c. 1920. In 1920 an ex-army hut was bought and erected in the back garden of 26 Steel Road, by the Slim family, and this was used until the new Church/Parish Hall (now the School Hall) was built in 1930. The church building was finally completed in 1936.

The interior of St Brigids church, 1936.

St Bartholomew's, Hoggs Lane, in the Allens Cross area of Northfield.

West Heath Mission church, later became St Anne's. When a new church was built, c. 1970, the original church building became the church hall.

Eight
Circling the Village

The Manor House, home of George and Elizabeth Cadbury. Later, part of the house was used as a hostel for nurses from the Woodlands, and is now accommodation for university students.

Traffic on the pre war Bristol Road South. The advert on the front of the tram is for Wheeler's garage in Northfield Village.

Shenley Lane in 1931, this is now a dual carriageway.

Merritts Brook Lane.

Ley Hill Estate Lodge, 1957. Now part of the Ley Hill Neighbourhood office.

Allens Cross housing estate built between the two world wars, 1948.

Hanging Lane, this connects Frankley Beeches Road with Tessall Lane. Despite its name this lane was not the site of a gallows, the name refers to way the road has been cut into the banks of rock.

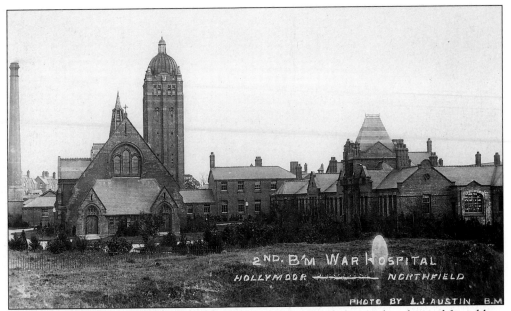

Hollymoor Hospital, *c.* 1940. The hospital was just one of many hospitals to be used for soldiers during the Second World War.

The Lodge and gateway to Hollymoor Hospital, *c.* 1940.

Cock Lane in 1933, later to be renamed Frankley Beeches Road, looking towards the Bristol Road from a point just above St Heliers Road.

This is the view from Cock Lane of the Bristol Road, and showing Mr Hands shop on the corner of Chatham Road, 1934.

Pigeon House Hill, *c.* 1900. The stretch of the Bristol Road between Hill Top Road and South Road was known originally as Pigeon House Hill, on the right of the picture is Pigeon House, a private school. The gates on the left lead to Hill Farm.

The Grange, which at one time was moated on three sides. The origin of this house is unknown although the oldest part was thought to be Elizabethan and therefore built between 1550 and 1600. The Grange was a farmhouse for many years but in the 1930s it became the home of Dr Foxwell. The building has now been replaced by the Longbridge Social Club.

The Bristol Road, *c.* 1945, from the junction of South Road looking towards Longbridge.

Pigeon House Hill, Bristol Road, 1905, viewed from the corner of Steel Road.

The Bristol Road South, *c.* 1924, showing the tram lines being laid.

Bristol Road South in September 1937, opposite Hawkesley Mill Lane looking towards Northfield Village.

Longbridge Lane as it crosses over the River Rea, 1922.

Longbridge Lane in 1932, showing the bridge over the River Rea.

Longbridge Place, the home of the Impey Family who founded Kalamazoo. The Greenlands Club is now on the same site.

Longbridge Lane in 1945.

The duck pond. It is believed that this pond was in Coombes Lane, c. 1925.

Grovelly Hall, close to the junction of Redditch Road with Longbridge Lane. The hall has survived on this site for more than 300 years, although there have been alterations and additions in that time and it is the original building that has survived. The hall and the estate surrounding it has been owned by numerous families including the Coombes, Lyttletons and Bournville Village Trust.

Tessall Lane, 1935, looking towards the Bristol Road, showing buildings which were formerly part of Tessall Farm.

The footbridge over the brook in Turves Green close to the junction with West Heath Road, 1937.

Turves Green viewed from West Heath Road in 1937, an old public footpath crosses the road.

Hawkesley Mill Lane, *c.* 1940

Kalamazoo Works, *c.* 1920. Kalamazoo, founded by Oliver Morland and F. Paul Impey, moved to Northfield in 1913, from Barwick Street. The factory was at first housed in an old brick works, but over the years a number of other buildings have been added.

Digbeth Mill Northfield, at the corner of Mill Lane and Quarry lane, *c.* 1900.

South Road, 1925, looking towards the station with farm land on the left.

The junction of South Road and Quarry Lane in 1925. This is now the entrance to the station and Copse Close.

Quarry House in Quarry Lane, 1937

Pamela Road, a photograph taken soon after the houses were completed. Note the young trees, c. 1935

The Old Tithe Barn, in Woodland Road. This was modernised and converted into a home in the 1950s but later in the 1970s it was demolished to make way for Pine Walk. The original building was Elizabethan, and lay just outside the churchyard where it was used to store 'tithes', paid to the church annually in the form of farm produce.

The Old Tithe Barn after conversion.

Nine
Northfield Farms

Ash Bank Farm. This farm was in the heart of Northfield, where today we find the MEB/Powerhouse.

Coombes Farm, Longbridge, c. 1919.

The rear of Coombes Farm. The rear of the farm house was of an earlier date than the front, and was believed to be Elizabethan.

Old Bell Farm with the farmyard at the rear. In 1910, Horace Satchwell lived here and is listed in directories as a cattle dealer .

Rear of Old Bell Farm.

One of four cottages in Bell Hill known as Paradise, *c.* 1905.

Hole Farm, the farm house can still be found in Hole Lane.

Hoggs Farm, c. 1900. Established by 1583 when fields were enclosed, but now this site lies under Frankley Reservoir.

A watercolour painting by Henry Hipsley of Staffords Farm, also known as Hawkesley Mill Farm. It was farmed by two generations of the Stafford family up till 1917 when the land was bought by Herbert Austin. The farm house was close to the site of the old laundry at the end of Mill Walk.

The farmer and his wife, Mr and Mrs E. Smith, of Frogmill Farm, pose for a photograph in 1900 with their pony and trap and two sporting spaniels. When Mr Smith died, his widow continued to run the farm until 1953 when she was 83. The farm was then sold

Ten

Longbridge
and West Heath

The junction of Bristol Road South and Lickey Road, 1923.

The junction of Bristol Road South and Lickey Road in the 1940s, now replaced by a traffic island. The Austin factory is on the right.

The Austin Works, c. 1910. Here we see a new model being test driven!

The junction of Longbridge Lane and Bristol Road South, September 1922. The placard on the corner is advertising a Tom Mix film, *The Marriage Cheat*.

Workers outside the Austin Works in 1922.

The track at the Austin Works, Longbridge, *c.* 1922.

Herbert Austin, later Lord Austin, driving an Austin Seven, *c.* 1925. Herbert Austin arrived in Longbridge in 1905 when he bought a disused printing works and started his first car factory. By 1910 he had 1,000 workers and the factory became the first in Britain to introduce, among other things, a night shift.

The Aero Works opposite Cofton Park, 1944. During the war the Austin Works was heavily involved in manufacturing parts for Spitfires, etc.

CENTRAL AVENUE.
2

The Austin Village in Central Avenue. Lord Austin had this 'village' of wooden bungalows built to house workers from the factory. The bungalows were imported from America in 1916.

Bungalows in Hawkesley Drive, *c.* 1920.

The Austin Village decorated for the 1918 victory celebrations, soon after completion. This estate is now a conservation area.

The corner of Low Hill Lane and Lickey Road, *c*. 1900.

The junction of Redhill Road and West Heath Road near the corner of the Fordrough, 1937.

The Fordrough viewed from the West Heath Road, *c.* 1925.

Alvechurch Road and Redhill Road, junction with West Heath Road, *c.* 1940.

West Heath Fete, *c.* 1923 held at The Hayes. The fete was opened by Canon Price, the vicar of Kings Norton. He stood on a cart supplied by Ernest Loxley, the monumental mason, who had a business on the corner of Frankley Beeches Road and Bristol Road.

The Bath Tub, Alvechurch Road, West Heath. The Bath Tub, an open air swimming pool, cafe and ballroom, was opened by Gracie Fields on 1 July 1937 at 9pm. It was estimated that over 20,000 people attended the opening. The ceremony was presided over by Ronald Cartland, MP for Kings Norton and Northfield (brother of Dame Barbara Cartland), and Mantovani, personally conducting his orchestra.

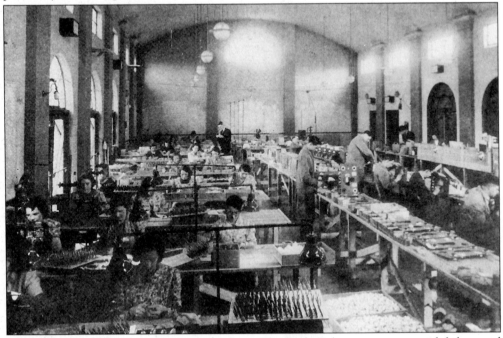

The Bath Tub after conversion into a factory. The Bath Tub was a commercial failure and closed within three years. Before decisions could be made about the conversion of the site, the Second World War intervened and the site was requisitioned in November 1940 and converted into a factory producing radio equipment.